by Iain Gray

WRITING *to* REMEMBER

WRITING *to* REMEMBER

79 Main Street, Newtongrange,
Midlothian EH22 4NA
Tel: 0131 344 0414   Fax: 0845 075 6085
E-mail: info@lang-syne.co.uk
www.langsyneshop.co.uk

Design by Dorothy Meikle
Printed by Printwell Ltd
© Lang Syne Publishers Ltd 2017

All rights reserved. No part of this publication may be reproduced, stored or introduced into a retrieval system, or transmitted in any form or by any means (electronic, mechanical, photocopying, recording or otherwise) without the prior written permission of Lang Syne Publishers Ltd.

ISBN 978-1-85217-325-8

Sweeney

MOTTO:
By the providence of God.

CREST:
An arm in armour holding a battle-axe
(senior line of the clan).

NAME variations include:
MacSuibhne (*Gaelic*)
MacSweeney
MacSweeny
MacSwiney
MacSwyn
MacSwyny
Sevnagh
Sweeny
Sweney
Swiney
MacQueen

Chapter one:
Origins of Irish surnames

According to an old saying, there are two types of Irish – those who actually are Irish and those who wish they were.

This sentiment is only one example of the allure that the high romance and drama of the proud nation's history holds for thousands of people scattered across the world today.

It's a sad fact, however, that the vast majority of Irish surnames are found far beyond Irish shores, rather than on the Emerald Isle itself.

The population stood at around eight million souls in 1841, but today it stands at fewer than six million.

This is mainly a tragic consequence of the potato famine, also known as the Great Hunger, which devastated Ireland between 1845 and 1849.

The Irish peasantry had become almost wholly reliant for basic sustenance on the potato, first introduced from the Americas in the seventeenth century.

When the crop was hit by a blight, at least 800,000 people starved to death while an estimated two million others were forced to seek a new life far from their native shores – particularly in America, Canada, and Australia.

The effects of the potato blight continued until about 1851, by which time a firm pattern of emigration had become established.

Ireland's loss, however, was to the gain of the countries in which the immigrants settled, contributing enormously, as their descendants do today, to the well being of the nations in which their forefathers settled.

But those who were forced through dire circumstance to establish a new life in foreign parts never forgot their roots, or the proud heritage and traditions of the land that gave them birth.

Nor do their descendants.

It is a heritage that is inextricably bound up in the colourful variety of Irish names themselves – and the origin and history of these names forms an integral part of the vibrant drama that is the nation's history, one of both glorious fortune and tragic misfortune.

This history is well documented, and one of the most important and fascinating of the earliest sources are *The Annals of the Four Masters*, compiled between 1632 and 1636 by four friars at the Franciscan Monastery in County Donegal.

Compiled from earlier sources, and purporting to go back to the Biblical Deluge, much of the material takes in the mythological origins and history of Ireland and the Irish.

This includes tales of successive waves of invaders and settlers such as the Fomorians, the Partholonians, the Nemedians, the Fir Bolgs, the Tuatha De Danann, and the Laigain.

Of particular interest are the *Milesian Genealogies*,

because the majority of Irish clans today claim a descent from either Heremon, Ir, or Heber – three of the sons of Milesius, a king of what is now modern day Spain.

These sons invaded Ireland in the second millennium B.C, apparently in fulfilment of a mysterious prophecy received by their father.

This Milesian lineage is said to have ruled Ireland for nearly 3,000 years, until the island came under the sway of England's King Henry II in 1171 following what is known as the Cambro-Norman invasion.

This is an important date not only in Irish history in general, but for the effect the invasion subsequently had for Irish surnames.

'Cambro' comes from the Welsh, and 'Cambro-Norman' describes those Welsh knights of Norman origin who invaded Ireland.

But they were invaders who stayed, inter-marrying with the native Irish population and founding their own proud dynasties that bore Cambro-Norman names such as Archer, Barbour, Brannagh, Fitzgerald, Fitzgibbon, Fleming, Joyce, Plunkett, and Walsh – to name only a few.

These 'Cambro-Norman' surnames that still flourish throughout the world today form one of the three main categories in which Irish names can be placed – those of Gaelic-Irish, Cambro-Norman, and Anglo-Irish.

Previous to the Cambro-Norman invasion of the twelfth century, and throughout the earlier invasions and settlement of those wild bands of sea rovers known as the Vikings in the eighth and ninth centuries, the population of the island was relatively small, and it was normal for a person to be identified through the use of only a forename.

But as population gradually increased and there were many more people with the same forename, surnames were adopted to distinguish one person, or one community, from another.

Individuals identified themselves with their own particular tribe, or 'tuath', and this tribe – that also became known as a clann, or clan – took its name from some distinguished ancestor who had founded the clan.

The Gaelic-Irish form of the name Kelly, for example, is Ó Ceallaigh, or O'Kelly, indicating descent from an original 'Ceallaigh', with the 'O' denoting 'grandson of.' The name was later anglicised to Kelly.

The prefix 'Mac' or 'Mc', meanwhile, as with the clans of the Scottish Highlands, denotes 'son of.'

Although the Irish clans had much in common with their Scottish counterparts, one important difference lies in what are known as 'septs', or branches, of the clan.

Septs of Scottish clans were groups who often bore an entirely different name from the clan name but were under the clan's protection.

In Ireland, septs were groups that shared the same name and who could be found scattered throughout the four provinces of Ulster, Leinster, Munster, and Connacht.

The 'golden age' of the Gaelic-Irish clans, infused as their veins were with the blood of Celts, pre-dates the Viking invasions of the eighth and ninth centuries and the Norman invasion of the twelfth century, and the sacred heart of the country was the Hill of Tara, near the River Boyne, in County Meath.

Known in Gaelic as 'Teamhar na Rí', or Hill of Kings, it was the royal seat of the 'Ard Rí Éireann', or High King of Ireland, to whom the petty kings, or chieftains, from the island's provinces were ultimately subordinate.

It was on the Hill of Tara, beside a stone pillar known as the Irish 'Lia Fáil', or Stone of Destiny, that the High Kings were inaugurated and, according to legend, this stone would emit a piercing screech that could be heard all over Ireland when touched by the hand of the rightful king.

The Hill of Tara is today one of the island's main tourist attractions.

Opposition to English rule over Ireland, established in the wake of the Cambro-Norman invasion, broke out frequently and the harsh solution adopted by the powerful forces of the Crown was to forcibly evict the native Irish from their lands.

These lands were then granted to Protestant colonists, or 'planters', from Britain.

Many of these colonists, ironically, came from Scotland and were the descendants of the original 'Scotti', or 'Scots', who gave their name to Scotland after migrating there in the fifth century A.D., from the north of Ireland.

Colonisation entailed harsh penal laws being imposed on the majority of the native Irish population, stripping them practically of all of their rights.

The Crown's main bastion in Ireland was Dublin and its environs, known as the Pale, and it was the dispossessed peasantry who lived outside this Pale, desperately striving to eke out a meagre living.

It was this that gave rise to the modern-day expression of someone or something being 'beyond the pale'.

Attempts were made to stamp out all aspects of the ancient Gaelic-Irish culture, to the extent that even to bear a Gaelic-Irish name was to invite discrimination.

This is why many Gaelic-Irish names were anglicised with, for example, and noted above, Ó Ceallaigh, or O'Kelly, being anglicised to Kelly.

Succeeding centuries have seen strong revivals of Gaelic-Irish consciousness, however, and this has led to many families reverting back to the original form of their name, while the language itself is frequently found on the fluent tongues of an estimated 90,000 to 145,000 of the island's population.

Ireland's turbulent history of religious and political strife is one that lasted well into the twentieth century, a landmark century that saw the partition of the island into the twenty-six counties of the independent Republic of

Ireland, or Eire, and the six counties of Northern Ireland, or Ulster.

Dublin, originally founded by Vikings, is now a vibrant and truly cosmopolitan city while the proud city of Belfast is one of the jewels in the crown of Ulster.

It was Saint Patrick who first brought the light of Christianity to Ireland in the fifth century A.D.

Interpretations of this Christian message have varied over the centuries, often leading to bitter sectarian conflict – but the many intricately sculpted Celtic Crosses found all over the island are symbolic of a unity that crosses the sectarian divide.

It is an image that fuses the 'old gods' of the Celts with Christianity.

All the signs from the early years of this new millennium indicate that sectarian strife may soon become a thing of the past – with the Irish and their many kinsfolk across the world, be they Protestant or Catholic, finding common purpose in the rich tapestry of their shared heritage.

Chapter two:
High Kings

Although it is no easy task to entangle the strands that contribute to the complex but colourful genealogy of proud bearers of the name of Sweeney, it is a rewarding experience when it is revealed how their Celtic blood is infused with that of ancient warrior kings.

The Gaelic-Irish form of the name is MacSuibhne, indicating 'son of Suibhne', while 'suibhne' indicates 'well-disposed' or 'pleasant.' The original Suibhne, or Suibne, from whom the Sweeneys are considered to have taken their name, was an early seventh century Ard Rí, or High King of Ireland, who was known as Suibhne Menn, or 'Sweeney the Renowned.'

But the Sweeney descent from Irish royalty goes back much further than Sweeney the Renowned – to no less a figure than Niall Noíghiallach, better known to posterity as the great warrior king Niall of the Nine Hostages.

The dramatic life and times of this ancestor of the Sweeneys are steeped in stirring Celtic myth and legend.

The youngest son of Eochaidh Mugmedon, King of the province of Connacht, his mother died in childbirth and he was brought up by his evil stepmother Mongfhinn who was determined that he should die.

She accordingly abandoned him naked on the Hill of Tara, inauguration site of the Ard Rí, but he was found by a wandering bard and taken back to his father.

One legend is that Mongfhinn sent Niall and his four brothers – Brian, Fiachra, Ailill, and Fergus – to a renowned prophet who was also a blacksmith to determine which of them would succeed their father as Ard Rí.

The blacksmith, known as Sitchin, set the lads a task by deliberately setting fire to his forge. Niall's brothers ran in and came out carrying the spearheads, fuel, hammers, and barrels of beer that they had rescued, but Niall staggered out clutching the heavy anvil so vital to the blacksmith's trade.

By this deed, Sitchin prophesied that Niall would be the one who would take on the glorious mantle of kingship.

Another prophetic incident occurred one day while Niall and his brothers were engaged in the hunt.

Thirsty from their efforts they encountered an ugly old woman who offered them water – but only in return for a kiss.

Three of the lads, no doubt repelled by her green teeth and scaly skin, refused. Fiachra pecked her lightly on the cheek and, by this act, she prophesied that he would one day reign at Tara – but only briefly.

The bold Niall, however, kissed her fully on the lips. The hag then demanded that he should now have full sexual intercourse with her and, undaunted, he did so.

Through this action she was suddenly transformed into a stunningly beautiful young woman known as Flaithius, or Royalty, who predicted that he would become the greatest High King of Ireland.

His stepmother Mongfhinn later tried to poison him, but accidentally took the deadly potion herself and died.

This legend relates to what was known as the Festival of Mongfhinn, or Feis na Samhan (the Feast of Samhain), because it was on the evening of October 31, on Samhain's Eve, that the poisoning incident is said to have taken place.

It was believed for centuries in Ireland that, on Samhain Eve, Mongfhinn's warped and wicked spirit would roam the land in hungry search of children's souls.

The Festival, or Feast, of Samhain, is today better known as Halloween.

Niall became Ard Rí in 379 A.D. and embarked on the series of military campaigns and other daring adventures that would subsequently earn him the title of Niall of the Nine Hostages.

The nine countries and territories into which he raided and took hostages for ransom were the four Irish provinces of Munster, Leinster, Connacht and Ulster, Britain and the territories of the Saxons, Morini, Picts, and Dalriads.

Niall's most famous hostage was a young lad known as Succat, son of Calpernius, a Romano-Briton who lived in the area of present day Milford Haven, on the Welsh coast.

Later known as Patricius, or Patrick, he became renowned as Ireland's patron saint, St. Patrick, responsible for bringing the light of Christianity to the island in the early years of the fifth century A.D.

Raiding in Gaul, in the area of Boulogne-sur-mer in

present day France, Niall was ambushed and killed by one of his treacherous subjects in 405 A.D.

But his legacy survived through the royal dynasties and clans founded by his brothers and sons – including his son Eoghain, who laid the foundations of the clan confederation known as the Cineal Eoghain.

Part of the northern Uí Neill, these clans included the Sweeneys, MacLachlans, MacEwens, O'Neills and others.

The main territory of the Sweeneys was in present day Co. Donegal, in the northern province of Ulster.

But a dispute within the family ranks in the early eleventh century, over the rights to the kingship of the Donegal area known as Aileach, finally led to one of the contenders, Anrathan, quitting Irish shores along with a number of followers.

Crossing the North Channel, they fetched up in present day Argyllshire, in the west of Scotland, and eventually amassed rich territories.

The main seat of these expatriate Irish Sweeneys became Knapdale, where they built Castle Sween and whose brooding ruins can be seen to this day.

By the late thirteenth and early fourteenth centuries Scotland had become a battleground because of rival claimants to the throne and the imperialist ambitions of England's King Edward I and, later, his son Edward II.

One of the foremost claimants to the Scottish Crown was Robert the Bruce, but he was not universally supported, and the Sweeneys were among those who opposed his ambitions. Bruce managed to seize the Crown and later consolidated his kingship after inflicting a celebrated defeat on an English army at the battle of Bannockburn, in the summer of 1314.

Not unexpectedly, the Sweeneys found themselves dispossessed as Bruce distributed their Argyllshire lands among those who had remained loyal to him.

The Sweeney clan chieftain in Scotland at this time was Murchadh Mear Suibhne – with 'Mear' rather alarmingly denoting 'Mad'. But, mad or not, Murchadh took the sensible step of accepting the blow to the Sweeney fortunes and literally turning his back on Scotland.

He and the large bulk of the clan accordingly set back off across the North Channel to resettle in the original Sweeney homeland of Donegal, rejoining their kinsfolk who had remained there.

But some Sweeneys chose to remain in Scotland, later becoming identified there with the proud clan of MacQueen – and that is why 'MacQueen' is recognised as one of the many spelling variations of the Sweeney name.

The main base of the Sweeneys now became established at Fanad, on a bank of the estuary of Lough Swilly.

It was from here that they flourished to such an extent that they gradually branched off into three important and powerful septs that were destined to play an important role throughout the future course of Ireland's turbulent history.

Chapter three:
Clan of the Battle-Axe

The three main septs of the Sweeneys were those of MacSuibhne Fanad, MacSuibhne Banagh and MacSuibhne na d'Tuatha – and this proliferation of septs explains why there are different crests on the family coat of arms.

But a main feature of all the coats of arms is a boar and a battle-axe, and the reason for the recurrent motif of the battle-axe is that the Sweeneys were so renowned for their skilful use of this deadly weapon that they were known as 'The Clan of the Battle-Axe.'

The sept of MacSuibhne Fanad, known as 'the chiefly family of Doe', is recognised as the senior line of the family, and it was at Fanad in Donegal that they built an imposing castle at Rathmullan in addition to a number of other castles that included that of Rahain, or Rahan.

The MacSuibhne Banagh sept sprang from the loins of Dubhgall, a grandson of Murchadh 'the Mad', while a branch of the MacSuibhne na d'Tuath sept relocated much further southwards from Donegal to the area of present day Co. Cork.

More than two centuries before these septs had become established, what proved to be the death knell of the ancient Gaelic-Irish way of life of clans such as the Sweeneys had been sounded.

This was in the form of the Norman invasion of Ireland and the subsequent consolidation of the power of the English Crown.

By 1175, English dominion over the island had been ratified through the Treaty of Windsor, under the terms of which Irish chieftains were only allowed to rule territory unoccupied by the Normans in the role of a vassal of the English monarch.

But the powerful Norman barons, not content with the land they already held, began to ruthlessly encroach on other lands as further hordes of land-hungry Anglo-Normans also descended on the island.

The Anglo-Norman family of de Burgh, or Burke, came to hold sway as Earls of Ulster, and *The Annals of the Four Masters* record how Murragh MacSweeney was thrown into prison by them – and it was here that he died in 1267.

The *Annals* also record the death in 1524 of Niall Mór MacSweeney, chief of the Branagh sept, and how he had been renowned not only for his leadership, prowess in battle and heroism, but also for his wisdom and generosity.

He was buried at Ballysaggart, at St. John's Point, but his magnificent headstone was later removed to St. Mary's Church in Killybegs, overlooking Donegal Bay, where it can be admired today.

Stoking the flames of the frequent rebellions that periodically erupted in Ireland against the English Crown was its policy of settling or 'planting' loyal Protestants on Irish land.

This policy had started during the reign from 1491 to 1547 of Henry VIII, whose Reformation effectively outlawed the established Roman Catholic faith throughout his dominions.

This settlement of loyal Protestants in Ireland continued throughout the subsequent reigns of Elizabeth I, James I (James VI of Scotland), and Charles I.

For many native Irish, any enemy of England was a friend of theirs, and in the late sixteenth century one of their greatest allies was England's deadliest foe – Spain.

A 130-strong Spanish fleet, intent on the invasion of the England of Queen Elizabeth I, was scattered in heavy storms after its defeat at the battle of Gravelines in the autumn of 1588, and many vessels were driven towards the west coast of Ireland.

This caused alarm on the part of the English authorities on the island, who feared, not without justification, that the disaffected native Irish would rally to their rescue.

William Fitzwilliam, Lord Deputy of Ireland, even sanctioned the use of torture against survivors, while also ordering that anyone who came to their aid would be declared traitors.

At least 24 Spanish vessels were wrecked on the Irish coastline – from Co. Antrim in the north of the island to Co. Kerry in the south.

One of the ships was *La Trinidad Valencera*, which had already taken on survivors of the shipwrecked *Barca de Amburgo*.

Grossly overladen and listing in heavy seas, the order was given to abandon ship as she lay in Glenagivney Bay, in Co. Donegal.

Up to 560 soaked and exhausted survivors managed to struggle ashore, but were intercepted by a heavily armed body of troops.

Trusting to the mercy of the authorities, they had no sooner surrendered their arms when the Spanish officers and noblemen were separated from the group and 300 of the ordinary seamen massacred on the spot.

About 150 survivors managed to flee the scene of carnage and, intercepted by sympathetic native Irish who included Eoghan Óg MacSweeney, the Chief of Doe, were given refuge until their escape from the island was arranged.

Rebellion erupted on the island in 1594 against the increasingly harsh treatment of the native Irish and at its forefront was the O'Donnell chieftain Aodh Rua ÓDomhmaill, better known to posterity as Red Hugh O'Donnell.

In what became known as the Cogadh na Naoi mBliama, or the Nine Years War, Red Hugh and his determined allies, who included Eoghan Óg MacSweeney's eldest son, also known as Eoghan, set the island ablaze in a vicious campaign of guerrilla warfare.

A whirlwind of devastation was wreaked on English settlements and garrisons in a daring series of lightning raids while, in 1596, allied with the forces of Hugh O'Neill, Earl of Tyrone, a defeat on an English army was inflicted at the battle of Clontibert.

This was followed by a significant victory for the rebels nearly two years later at the battle of Yellow Ford.

But the most significant defeat inflicted on the English forces during the Nine Years War came at the battle of Curlew Pass, fought on August 15th, 1599, near Boyle, Co. Roscommon, in the northwest of the island.

With Eoghan Óg MacSweeney in command of the rebel vanguard, the rebels ambushed an English force under the command of Sir Conyers Clifford at a pass through the imposing Curlew Mountains and routed them.

The English lost at least 500 men, including Clifford, whose head was cut off and triumphantly given to Red Hugh.

As English control over Ireland teetered on the brink of collapse, thousands more troops were hastily despatched and, in the face of the overwhelming odds against them, Red Hugh and the Earl of Tyrone sought help from Spain.

A well-equipped Spanish army under General del Aquila landed at Kinsale in December of 1601, but was forced into surrender only a few weeks later, in January of 1602.

It was Eoghan Óg's kinsman, Sir Miles MacSweeney,

who fought in the bitter rearguard action in the rebel retreat from Kinsale.

Resistance continued until 1603, but proved abortive and Red Hugh O'Donnell had already been forced to flee to Spain.

Four years later, in September of 1607 and in what is known as The Flight of the Earls, Hugh O'Neill, 2nd Earl of Tyrone and Rory O'Donnell, 1st Earl of Tyrconnel, sailed into foreign exile from the village of Rathmullan, on the shore of Lough Swilly, in the Sweeney homeland of Co. Donegal, accompanied by ninety loyal followers.

But Eoghan Óg MacSweeney was not among their number.

He had been captured and imprisoned two years earlier and told that his life would be spared if he revealed what he knew of Rory O'Donnell's activities.

Opting for death rather than the betrayal of O'Donnell, he was executed in Lifford Castle in May of 1605.

Sweeneys were also at the heart of subsequent eruptions of warfare that devastated the island and further eroded their ancient Gaelic-Irish way of life.

The final nail in their coffin, and that of other clans, came in the aftermath of what is known in Ireland as Cogadh an Dá Rí, or The War of the Two Kings.

Also known as the Williamite War in Ireland, it was ignited when the Stuart monarch James II, under threat from powerful factions who feared a return to the dominance of Roman Catholicism under his rule, fled into French exile in 1688.

The Protestant William of Orange and his wife Mary were invited to take up the throne – but James had significant Catholic support in Ireland.

These supporters were known as Jacobites, and among them were Donough Óge MacSweeney, the 13th chief of the clan, and his uncle Edmund MacSweeney.

James, with the support of troops and money supplied by Louis XIV of France, had landed at Kinsale in March of 1689 and joined forces with his Irish supporters.

A series of military encounters followed, culminating in James's defeat by an army commanded by William at the battle of the Boyne on July 12, 1690.

James fled again into French exile and, after another series of military encounters, Jacobite defeat was finally ratified through the Treaty of Limerick.

Prominent on the 'Most Wanted' list of particularly recalcitrant Jacobites were Donough Óge MacSweeney and his uncle.

Both men reluctantly left their native land for France, where they died in lonely exile.

Chapter four:
On the world stage

Bearers of the proud name of Sweeney have gained international recognition through their participation in a wide range of pursuits.

Born in 1961 on Long Island, New York, Daniel Bernard Sweeney is the American stage, film and television actor better known as **D.B. Sweeney**.

In addition to his roles in American television series such as the medical drama *House*, he has also appeared in films that include the 1987 *Gardens of Stone*, the 1990 *Memphis Belle* and the 2001 *Hardball*.

Born in Philadelphia in 1884, **Joseph Sweeney** was the American television and movie actor whose most memorable role was as 'Juror No. 9' in the 1957 courtroom drama *12 Angry Men*.

Other roles include the 1936 *Soak the Rich* and the 1956 *The Man in the Grey Flannel Suit*.

Creator and performer of the autobiographical monologues *God Said Ha!*, *In the Family Way* and *Letting Go of God*, **Julia Sweeney** is the American actress and comedian born in 1959 in Spokane, Washington.

A consultant to television dramas such as *Sex and the City* and *Desperate Housewives*, she has also appeared in television comedies that include *Frasier* and films that include *Pulp Fiction* and *Clockstoppers*.

Born in 1971 in Liverpool, **Claire Sweeney** is the English actress, singer and television personality who first rose to fame on the British television soap *Brookside*, while **Bob Sweeney** was a leading American actor, director and producer of radio, television and film.

Born in 1918 in San Francisco, he first achieved fame in the mid-1940s along with Hal March as one of the *Sweeney and March* CBS radio comedy duo.

His notable film roles include director John Ford's 1958 *The Last Hurrah* and Alfred Hitchcock's 1964 *Marnie*, while he also produced popular television shows that included *Hawaii Five-O* and *The Love Boat*.

He died in 1992.

Born in Los Angeles in 1976, **Alison Sweeney** is the American actress best known for her role in the television soap *Days of Our Lives*, while behind the camera lens **Mary Sweeney** is the award-winning American film editor and producer who was born in 1948.

The partner of film director David Lynch, she has collaborated with him on a number of television series and films that include *Twin Peaks*, the 1997 *Lost Highway* and the 2001 *Mulholland Drive*.

In the world of music, **Joel Sweeney**, who was also known as Joe Sweeney, was the American musician and 'blackface minstrel' who was born in 1810 in Virginia and who died in 1860.

Learning to play the banjo from local African-Americans as a young man, he is believed to have been one of the earliest documented white players of the instrument.

Sweeney, who toured Europe in the early 1940s as part of the Virginia Minstrels, is also recognised as having done much to not only popularise the banjo but also to have assisted in the development of what has become the modern five-string banjo.

In contemporary times, **William Sweeney** is the Scottish composer who was born in 1950 in Glasgow and whose orchestral works, influenced by traditional folk music, include the 1984 *Magam* and the 1996 *Sweeney Astray*.

Born in 1920 in Montreal, **Daisy Sweeney** is the married name of the accomplished Canadian music teacher Daisy Peterson.

A sister of jazz pianist Oscar Peterson, she is best known for having taught leading Canadian jazz musicians who include Joe Sealy, Oliver Jones, Ken Skinner and Reg Wilson.

She is also the mother of the Canadian journalist and television producer and former women's baseball star **Sylvia Sweeney**.

Born in 1956 in Montreal, she was a member of Canada's women's basketball team at both the 1976 and 1984 Olympics.

Entering the world of journalism in the late 1980s, she later became noted for her work in the television production

In the Key of Oscar – a documentary about Oscar Peterson, her uncle.

An annual Sylvia Sweeney Award is made to the Canadian women's university basketball player who best exemplifies the values of athletics, academics and community involvement.

In baseball, **Edward Sweeney**, born in 1888 in Chicago, was the Major League Baseball catcher who played for the New York Yankees from 1908 to 1915, while William Sweeney was a an infielder in Major League.

Born in 1886 in Covington, Kentucky, teams he played for between 1907 and 1914 included the Chicago Cubs and the Boston Doves.

In the equally competitive sport of ice hockey, **Bill Sweeney**, born in 1937 in Guelph, Ontario was a professional player from 1957 to 1969.

Teams he played for included the New York Rangers and the Vancouver Canucks.

Also in ice hockey, **Don Sweeney** is the former player who was born in 1966 in St. Stephen, New Brunswick, and who played for the Boston Bruins of the National Hockey League.

In the sport of lacrosse, **Kyle Sweeney**, born in 1981 in Springfield, Philadelphia, is the player who represented the U.S.A. in the 2007 World Indoor Lacrosse Championship.

In the strenuous sport of rowing, **Patrick Sweeney**, born in 1952, is the British rower whose many achievements include winning a bronze medal, along with Sir Stephen Redgrave and Andy Holmes, at the 1988 Olympics.

In the world of art, **James Sweeney**, born in 1900 and who died in 1986, was the American curator and expert on modern art who acted in the late 1960s as a consultant to the National Gallery of Australia.

In the world of fiction, **Sweeney Todd** is the frightening character who was first introduced to the reading public in *The String of Pearls* series of tales between 1846 and 1847.

A barber with premises in London's Fleet Street, he is reputed to have murdered his hapless customers by slitting their throats with a razor and, in a further gruesome twist, then having their remains turned into meat pies.

His exploits have also been adapted for the screen, most recently in the 2007 *Sweeney Todd: The Demon Barber of Fleet Street*, with Johnny Depp in the title role.

On the field of battle, **Major General Charles Sweeney**, born in 1919 in Lowell, Massachusetts was an officer with the United States Army Air Force (USAAF) during the Second World War.

Joining the air corps in 1941, by 1944 he had been promoted to Major and assigned as a B-29 Superfortress pilot instructor.

But it was on August 9 of 1945 that he entered the history books – as the pilot who dropped the 'Fat Boy' atomic bomb on the Japanese city of Nagasaki. He died in 2004.

Born in 1853, **Robert Sweeney** served in the United

States Navy and became one of only 19 servicemen, and the only African-American, to receive the distinguished Medal of Honor twice for peacetime actions.

His first medal citation was for rescuing a shipmate who had fallen overboard in October of 1881, while the second came following a similar incident that occurred seven years before his death in 1890.

It was only through a cruel twist of fate that Madeline Amy Sweeney, who was better known as **Amy Sweeney**, became both a victim and a heroine of the 9/11 attacks on New York's World Trade Center in 2001.

Born in 1966 and a native of Massachusetts, she had been a flight attendant on board American Airlines Flight II when it was flown by terrorist hijackers into the north tower.

Married with two children then aged four and six, she normally only worked weekends, but had been asked by her employers to take on an extra shift on that fateful day of September 11 because one of the assigned crew members would be absent due to illness.

During the hijacking of the aircraft she relayed information by airfone to the flight operations centre on what was happening before the plane hit the north tower.

A flight attendant for 12 years, she had lived with her husband and children in Acton, Massachusetts, and it was in her honour that in February of 2002 the annual Madeline Amy Sweeney Award for Civilian Bravery was instituted by the State of Massachusetts.

Awarded to the Massachusetts citizen who displays extraordinary courage in defending or saving the lives of others, its first recipients were Amy, fellow flight attendant Betty Ong and pilot John Ogonowski – who had also relayed important information on the hijackers to airline staff on the ground.

The actress Irene Carl has since memorably portrayed Amy Sweeney in the moving television drama-documentary *The Last Hour of Flight 11*.

Key dates in Ireland's history from the first settlers to the formation of the Irish Republic:

circa 7000 B.C.	Arrival and settlement of Stone Age people.
circa 3000 B.C.	Arrival of settlers of New Stone Age period.
circa 600 B.C.	First arrival of the Celts.
200 A.D.	Establishment of Hill of Tara, Co. Meath, as seat of the High Kings.
circa 432 A.D.	Christian mission of St. Patrick.
800-920 A.D.	Invasion and subsequent settlement of Vikings.
1002 A.D.	Brian Boru recognised as High King.
1014	Brian Boru killed at battle of Clontarf.
1169-1170	Cambro-Norman invasion of the island.
1171	Henry II claims Ireland for the English Crown.
1366	Statutes of Kilkenny ban marriage between native Irish and English.
1529-1536	England's Henry VIII embarks on religious Reformation.
1536	Earl of Kildare rebels against the Crown.
1541	Henry VIII declared King of Ireland.
1558	Accession to English throne of Elizabeth I.
1565	Battle of Affane.
1569-1573	First Desmond Rebellion.
1579-1583	Second Desmond Rebellion.
1594-1603	Nine Years War.
1606	Plantation' of Scottish and English settlers.
1607	Flight of the Earls.
1632-1636	Annals of the Four Masters compiled.
1641	Rebellion over policy of plantation and other grievances.
1649	Beginning of Cromwellian conquest.
1688	Flight into exile in France of Catholic Stuart monarch James II as Protestant Prince William of Orange invited to take throne of England along with his wife, Mary.
1689	William and Mary enthroned as joint monarchs; siege of Derry.
1690	Jacobite forces of James defeated by William at battle of the Boyne (July) and Dublin taken.

Key dates

1691	Athlone taken by William; Jacobite defeats follow at Aughrim, Galway, and Limerick; conflict ends with Treaty of Limerick (October) and Irish officers allowed to leave for France.
1695	Penal laws introduced to restrict rights of Catholics; banishment of Catholic clergy.
1704	Laws introduced constricting rights of Catholics in landholding and public office.
1728	Franchise removed from Catholics.
1791	Foundation of United Irishmen republican movement.
1796	French invasion force lands in Bantry Bay.
1798	Defeat of Rising in Wexford and death of United Irishmen leaders Wolfe Tone and Lord Edward Fitzgerald.
1800	Act of Union between England and Ireland.
1803	Dublin Rising under Robert Emmet.
1829	Catholics allowed to sit in Parliament.
1845-1849	The Great Hunger: thousands starve to death as potato crop fails and thousands more emigrate.
1856	Phoenix Society founded.
1858	Irish Republican Brotherhood established.
1873	Foundation of Home Rule League.
1893	Foundation of Gaelic League.
1904	Foundation of Irish Reform Association.
1913	Dublin strikes and lockout.
1916	Easter Rising in Dublin and proclamation of an Irish Republic.
1917	Irish Parliament formed after Sinn Fein election victory.
1919-1921	War between Irish Republican Army and British Army.
1922	Irish Free State founded, while six northern counties remain part of United Kingdom as Northern Ireland, or Ulster; civil war up until 1923 between rival republican groups.
1949	Foundation of Irish Republic after all remaining constitutional links with Britain are severed.